Disney PRINCESS

Princess
The Essential Guide

WRITTEN BY

Naia Bray-Moffatt and
Catherine Saunders

We're together now.
Everything's going
to be fine, you'll see.

Princess
The Essential Guide

Contents

If you keep on believing, the dreams that you wish will come true.

Introduction

B Y ROYAL DECREE you are cordially invited to visit some far-off lands and meet some fabulous princesses. Be prepared for tales of magic spells, amazing courage, special friendships, and, of course, true love. You will discover that being a princess is not just about wearing beautiful dresses and falling in love with handsome princes—although that is the fun part!

G ET TO KNOW gentle Snow White,
sweet Aurora, caring Cinderella,
adventurous Ariel, kind Belle, feisty
Jasmine, brave Mulan, headstrong
Pocahontas, busy Tiana, and magical
Rapunzel. Step inside the princesses'
lives and learn all about the things they
love to do. Meet their beloved families,
closest friends, and worst enemies.
Join them on some fantastic adventures
in search of their happy ever after
and enter some magical worlds
where dreams really do come true!

Pocahontas

Rapunzel

Cinderella

Snow White

Aurora

Jasmine

Ariel

Mulan

Tiana

Belle

9

Snow White

*O*nce upon a time in a magical land there lived a beautiful young princess with hair as black as ebony, lips as red as roses and skin as white as snow. Her name was Snow White. Everyone loved Snow White, apart from her wicked stepmother, the Queen, who was jealous of Snow White's beauty.

Some day my prince will come.

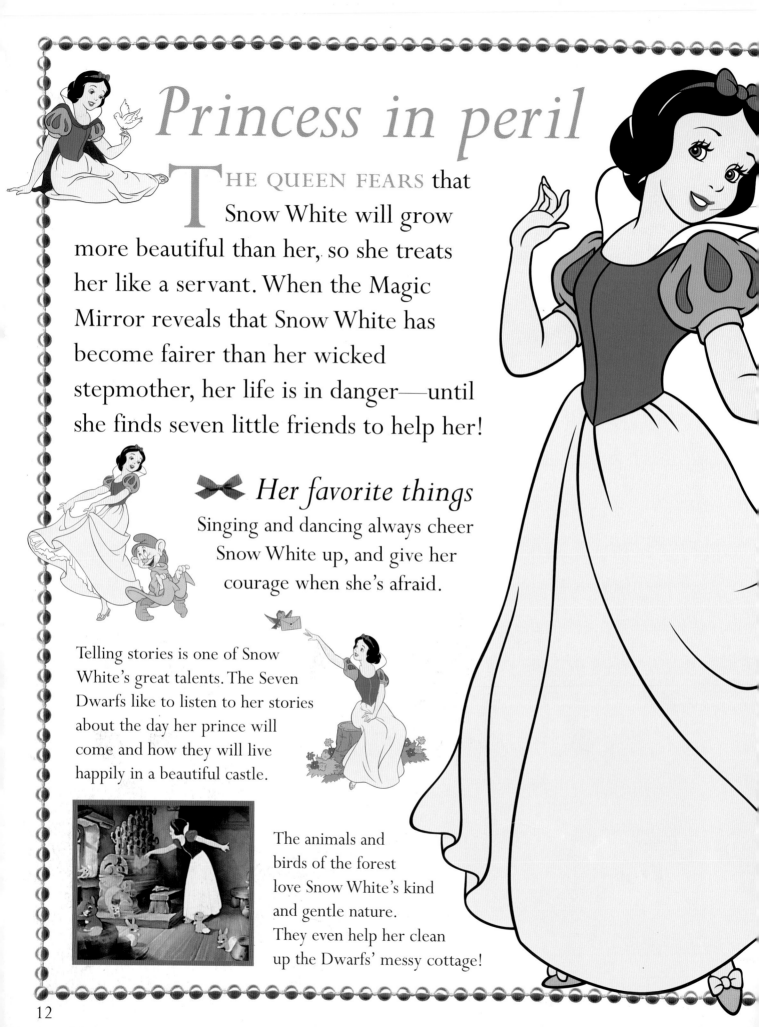

Princess in peril

THE QUEEN FEARS that Snow White will grow more beautiful than her, so she treats her like a servant. When the Magic Mirror reveals that Snow White has become fairer than her wicked stepmother, her life is in danger—until she finds seven little friends to help her!

Her favorite things

Singing and dancing always cheer Snow White up, and give her courage when she's afraid.

Telling stories is one of Snow White's great talents. The Seven Dwarfs like to listen to her stories about the day her prince will come and how they will live happily in a beautiful castle.

The animals and birds of the forest love Snow White's kind and gentle nature. They even help her clean up the Dwarfs' messy cottage!

Her hair is as black as ebony.

Her lips are as red as roses.

The lining of her sleeves match her hair ribbon.

ABOUT SNOW WHITE

♥ She's so sweet and gentle, she makes lots of friends wherever she goes.
♥ She is always cheerful and looks on the bright side.
♥ She is romantic and longs to meet her true love.
♥ She is practical and works hard.

Snow White sews her own petticoats to wear underneath her dresses.

Snow White loves to walk in the Enchanted Forest and pick the pretty flowers. But she can't bring too many into the cottage because flowers make Sneezy sneeze!

When the Dwarfs find out that Snow White is a good cook, they are delighted. Even more so when they discover she can bake their favorite gooseberry pie!

Oh, it's adorable!

❈ Love and romance

It seems like Snow White's wish for love will never come true, spending all her time working hard for the Queen.

But love always finds a way and even in her tattered rags, the Prince is captivated by Snow White's beauty.

Snow White's world

SNOW WHITE LIVES IN AN ENCHANTED land with seven jeweled hills and seven waterfalls. Beyond the farthest hill stands the castle where she grew up with her wicked stepmother, the Queen. From here you can see the pretty little cottage where the Seven Dwarfs live.

Running away

In the Dark Forest, even the trees seem to be against Snow White as she runs away from the Queen.

Snow White has nowhere to go and gets lost in the dense forest. Eventually she can run no farther and she falls to the ground in tears.

In disguise, the Queen sets off by boat to find Snow White.

The Queen's laboratory and dungeons lie below the castle.

The clearing where Snow White meets the friendly forest animals

The Prince

More than anything, Snow White longs for her Prince to carry her away to his castle, where they will live happily ever after.

The seven hills really are jeweled because there are dazzling diamonds inside. The Seven Dwarfs love to dig, dig, dig all day long in the mines.

The Prince's castle

The evil Queen tries to use the rock to stop the Dwarfs.

Entrance to the mines

The Enchanted Forest where Snow White sleeps in a glass coffin.

The cottage

The Seven Dwarfs are not very good at keeping their home clean and tidy! Snow White hopes to surprise them and cleans the cottage with some help from her little animal friends.

The Dwarfs' cottage

Friends and enemies

ONE OF THE GREAT GIFTS Snow White has is the ability to make friends easily; the animals and Dwarfs would do anything for her. Even Grumpy! But the Queen is madly jealous of her naturally beautiful stepdaughter. And the cruel Queen is a very dangerous enemy to have.

Her enemies

As well as being Snow White's stepmother, the Queen is also a wicked witch. She hates Snow White so much that she uses a poisoned apple to try and get rid of her.

'Magic Mirror on the wall, who is the fairest one of all?'

The Magic Mirror must answer all the questions that the jealous Queen asks.

Despite being pure evil, the Queen has a cold beauty.

The poisoned apple

Before turning red, for a moment the apple reveals the poison that covers it.

Although the Huntsman is a loyal servant of the Queen, he is not really wicked. Seeing Snow White's sweet nature, he cannot bear to carry out the Queen's order to kill the innocent princess.

Her friends

The Seven Dwarfs and the birds and animals that meet Snow White love her dearly. They try to protect her from the wicked Queen and her evil spells.

Grumpy   Doc   Bashful   Sneezy   Happy   Dopey   Sleepy

A wish comes true

From the moment that Snow White becomes more beautiful than the Queen, her life is in danger. Although the Seven Dwarfs try their best, they cannot protect her from the Queen's black magic. But good is stronger than evil, and in the end the Prince's love for Snow White saves the day.

✖ One spring morning

Snow White sings while she cleans. The Prince hears her and falls in love.

I beg of you, your Highness, forgive me!

The Magic Mirror tells the Queen that Snow White is the fairest in the land. The Queen orders the Huntsman to take the princess out to pick flowers in the forest and kill her.

Although he tries, the Huntsman can't bring himself to harm her and tells Snow White to run away. She flees and hides in the little cottage in the forest.

The cottage is owned by the Seven Dwarfs. When they come home to find a stranger in their home, they are afraid. But as soon as they meet Snow White, they want her to stay with them forever.

The poisoned apple

Disguised as an ugly old peddler woman, the Queen persuades trusting Snow White to take one bite of the poisoned apple. She promises this will make all her dreams come true.

No harm can come to Snow White now that her Prince has come.

There's nobody like him anywhere at all.

As soon as Snow White takes a bite of the apple, she falls to the ground in a deep sleep and cannot be woken. When the Dwarfs find her they place her in a special glass coffin, and keep a vigil at her side.

The Prince finds Snow White in the forest and wakes her from her slumber with true love's kiss. They set off for his palace and a future filled with happiness.

Cinderella

*O*nce upon a time a young girl lived happily with her father, stepmother, and stepsisters. One sad day the girl's father died, leaving her stepmother in charge. Before she knew it, the girl was forced to work as a servant to her stepmother and stepsisters. She became known as Cinderella.

Why, it's like a dream.
A wonderful dream
come true.

Servant girl

FROM THE MOMENT HER BELOVED FATHER dies, Cinderella's life changes forever. Her cruel Stepmother and spoiled stepsisters make her life miserable, but she never stops hoping and believing that one day her life will change and a handsome prince will sweep her off her feet.

ABOUT CINDERELLA

♥ She is cheerful and sunny, no matter how difficult things are.

♥ Cinderella is hard-working and practical and can cook and sew.

♥ She is very caring, and her heart is full of kindness.

Her friends

Although they are only tiny mice, Gus and Jaq are Cinderella's loyal friends. They help with her chores and save her from being lonely.

The Fairy Godmother makes Cinderella's dreams of happiness come true. Her magic spell makes it possible for Cinderella to go to the ball, even if it is only for a few hours.

Delicate lace petticoat

The long, flowing skirt, made of shimmering sky-blue satin, reflects the color of her eyes.

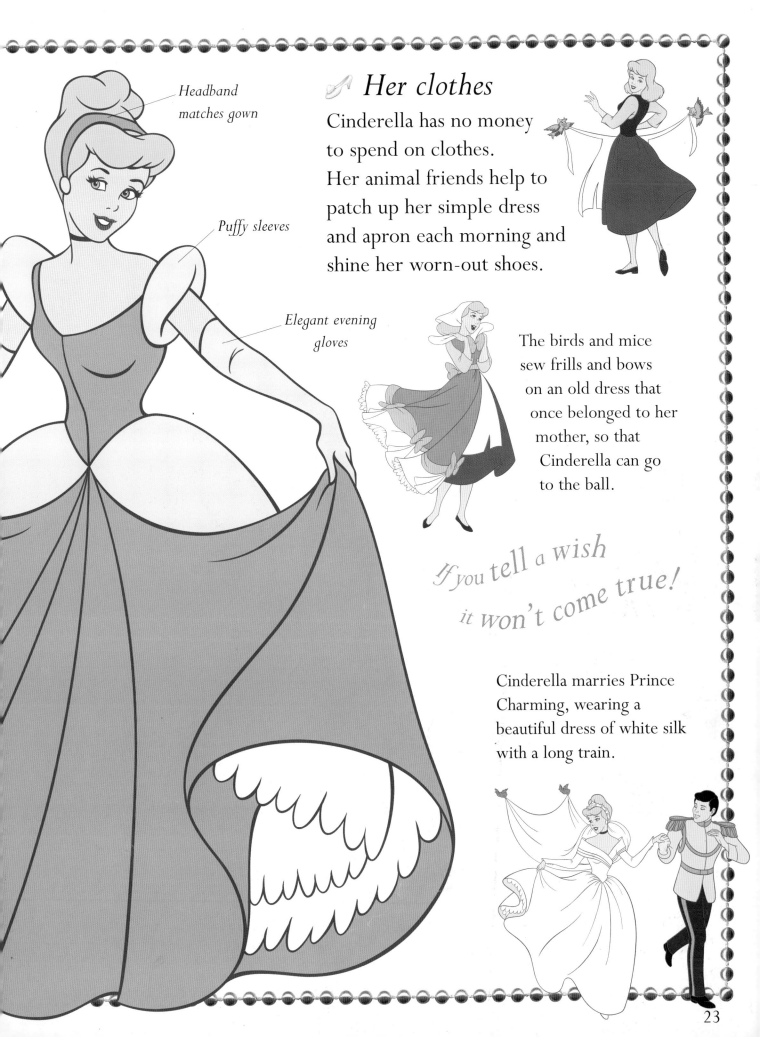

Headband matches gown

Puffy sleeves

Elegant evening gloves

♪ Her clothes

Cinderella has no money to spend on clothes. Her animal friends help to patch up her simple dress and apron each morning and shine her worn-out shoes.

The birds and mice sew frills and bows on an old dress that once belonged to her mother, so that Cinderella can go to the ball.

If you tell a wish it won't come true!

Cinderella marries Prince Charming, wearing a beautiful dress of white silk with a long train.

Home sweet home

ONCE UPON A TIME, the manor house was the happiest place in the whole of the kingdom. But when Cinderella's mean Stepmother arrives, things change. Lady Tremaine makes Cinderella sleep in the attic and do household chores all day long.

Cinderella's tiny attic bedroom

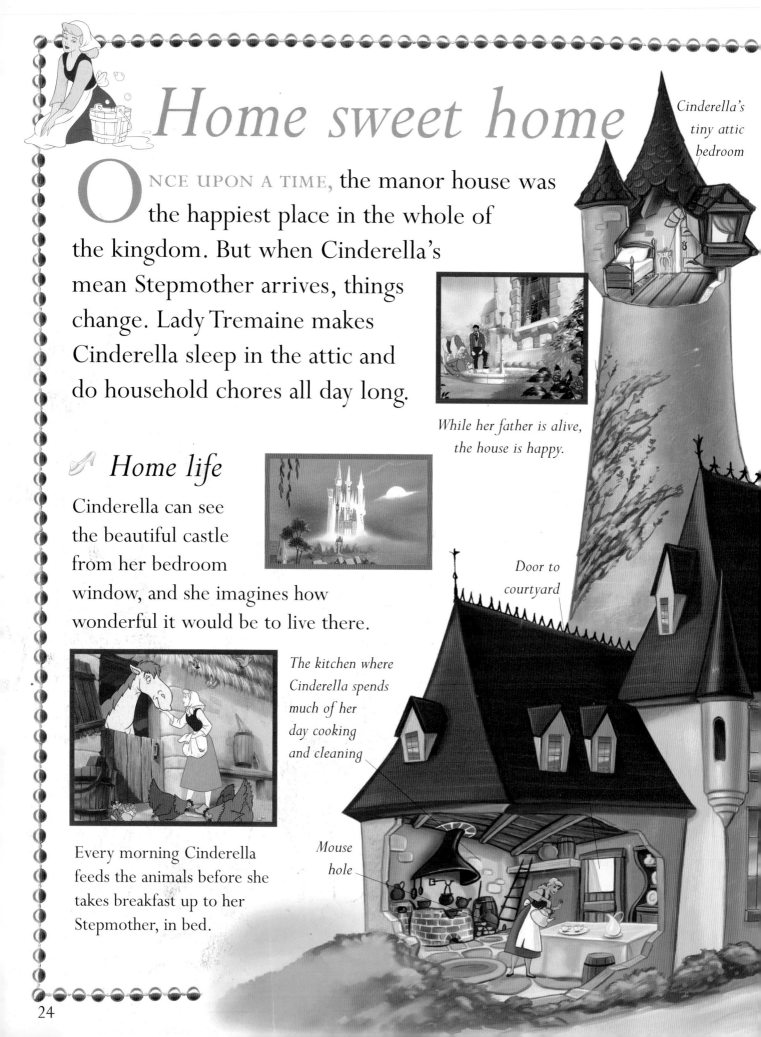

While her father is alive, the house is happy.

Home life

Cinderella can see the beautiful castle from her bedroom window, and she imagines how wonderful it would be to live there.

Every morning Cinderella feeds the animals before she takes breakfast up to her Stepmother, in bed.

The kitchen where Cinderella spends much of her day cooking and cleaning

Door to courtyard

Mouse hole

Family and friends

Jaq and Gus care deeply for Cinderella. The same cannot be said for her family; she waits on them hand and foot without any thanks!

Lady Tremaine and her spoiled daughters, Drizella and Anastasia, hate Cinderella because of her natural beauty.

Doors to Drizella and Anastasia's grand bedrooms

Lady Tremaine's bedroom is three times bigger than Cinderella's attic room.

Lucifer's velvet bed

Lucifer the cat lies in wait for the mice to torment them. Even Cinderella, who loves most animals, hasn't a good word to say about him!

Music room

Magic moments

A LITTLE MAGIC IS ALL Cinderella needs to find happiness after her father dies. She has charm and beauty, and all the elegance of a princess, and with a little help from her Fairy Godmother her dreams come true.

The invitation

To celebrate the Prince's return, all eligible ladies in the land are invited to attend a ball at the castle.

Cinderella's ugly stepsisters cannot bear to see her looking so beautiful in her mother's dress. They are so jealous they tear her outfit to pieces.

With a wave of her magic wand, the Fairy Godmother ensures that Cinderella can go to the ball.

👠 The ball

As soon as their eyes meet at the ball, Cinderella and the Prince fall in love. But when the clock strikes twelve, Cinderella leaves her glass slipper behind on the stairs in her hurry to leave before the magic ends. Soon her dress turns into rags.

Cinderella's golden hair is swept up on her head and she looks like a real princess.

The Grand Duke is absolutely delighted when Cinderella produces the matching glass slipper and slips it on to her dainty foot. Lady Tremaine, on the other hand, is furious.

Magic is in the air!

👠 The wedding

After all his searching, Prince Charming has at last found the beautiful girl he danced with at the ball. The whole kingdom rejoices when he marries Cinderella.

Sleeping Beauty

*I*n a far away land there lived a king and queen who longed to have a child. After many years their wish was granted with the birth of a daughter who they named Aurora. When an evil fairy placed a curse on the young princess, her parents sent her to live with the good fairies in the woods. The fairies renamed the girl Briar Rose.

Well, I'm really not supposed to speak to strangers, but we've met before.

Hidden princess

BROUGHT UP IN THE COUNTRYSIDE, this sweet and gentle girl has no idea that she is really a princess named Aurora. She learns the truth on her sixteenth birthday, the same day that, due to a curse put on her by a wicked fairy, she falls into an enchanted sleep. Only true love's first kiss saves her from eternal slumber.

Her favorite things

As a baby, Aurora was given the gift of song. Her voice is sweet and pure, and she loves to sing to the animals in the forest.

Aurora lives in a cottage situated in the heart of a beautiful forest. The woods are her playground where she can think and dream, dip her toes in the stream, and pick sweet berries.

ABOUT AURORA

♥ She's gentle and sweet-natured. All who know her love her.
♥ Aurora is thoughtful and unspoiled. She is always willing to help.
♥ She is a romantic and believes that her dreams of love will one day come true.

It takes lots of magic to create this beautiful dress, fit for a very special princess.

Her hair is the color of golden sunshine.

She is always ready with a smile.

Her beauty is as natural as a rose in bloom.

🌹 Her clothes

Growing up in the forest, Aurora has a simple wardrobe, but she is so unspoiled that she doesn't mind. And she is so beautiful that she looks lovely even in the plainest of dresses with just a shawl to wrap around her shoulders.

If you dream a thing more than once, it's sure to come true!

The good fairies use their magic to make Aurora a stunning birthday dress. But should it be pink or blue? They just can't decide on the color!

🌹 Her princess dress

When Aurora wears the magical dress and her golden crown, she is transformed from a sheltered young girl into an elegant princess. Now she is ready to marry Prince Phillip and become a beautiful bride.

31

Forest life

THE GOOD FAIRIES TAKE BABY AURORA to live in a pretty little cottage, deep in the forest, to hide her from the wicked fairy's curse. They rename her Briar Rose after the wild flower that grows in the forest, and they live here happily for sixteen years.

Birthday celebrations

Unlike most princesses, who have servants, Briar Rose begins her birthday by helping her aunts to dust and spring-clean their little cottage!

Flora, Fauna, and Merryweather love Briar Rose dearly and have special plans for her birthday. They ask her to pick berries in the forest so that they can make her a surprize gift.

Briar Rose meets the man of her dreams in the forest and her birthday is the happiest ever. She doesn't realize that the handsome young man is actually a prince.

The bed curtains come from the palace.

The little birds love to visit Briar Rose in her bedroom.

The sound of trickling water lulls Briar Rose to sleep at night.

Sparks of blue and pink magic escape from the chimney.

The roof is made of straw.

Merryweather

Fauna

Flora

The chamber where Aurora sleeps peacefully

Her bed is draped in rich velvet.

The spiral staircase leads to the secret chamber.

Castle life

NAMED AURORA AFTER THE DAWN because like a new day, she brought sunshine into her proud parents' lives, the baby princess seemed to have all she could wish for. But not for long! At the party given to celebrate her birth, the wicked fairy, Maleficent, promised that Aurora would prick her finger on a spindle and die before the sun set on her sixteenth birthday.

Baby celebrations

Flora and Fauna bless Aurora with gifts of song and beauty. But Merryweather still has her gift to give when Maleficent arrives.

At the party, King Hubert and King Stefan celebrate the betrothal of their children, Phillip and Aurora.

The good fairies rush to try and save Aurora.

The fire dies down to reveal a secret door to the tower.

Prince Phillip is the only one who can wake Aurora.

Maleficent is very offended when she is not invited to the royal party. She is so angry that she curses the baby Aurora. But luckily Merryweather has one gift to give and lessens the curse.

Sixteen years later

Maleficent's curse comes true when Aurora pricks her finger on a spinning wheel and falls into a deep sleep. When Prince Phillip tries to save Aurora, Maleficent turns into a fierce dragon—but with the Sword of Truth and Shield of Virtue he defeats her.

Sleeping Beauty

As far as Aurora is concerned, her life has been uneventful. For sixteen years she has lived in the forest longing for excitement and romance, with no friends other than the woodland animals. Then, on her sixteenth birthday, everything seems to happen at once!

The early years

Aurora's life changes forever when Maleficent arrives at the royal party and casts her evil spell.

Briar Rose meets Phillip whilst picking berries in the forest. The handsome young prince is the man of her dreams and they fall head-over-heels in love with each other.

Briar Rose is upset when the fairies tell her that she is a princess. She doesn't want to marry a prince she has never met! She doesn't realize that the prince she is to marry is the man she loves.

✺ Her birthday

As soon as Aurora pricks her finger on the spindle, she feels dizzy and sinks into a deep sleep.

We've met before.

Once upon a dream!

When the fairies find Aurora asleep, they know that the King and Queen will be heartbroken.

When Phillip kisses Aurora, Maleficent's curse is broken and she wakes from her sleep.

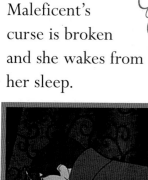

Prince Phillip can't take his eyes off the beautiful princess.

The precious golden crown is a present from the good fairies.

The floaty skirt makes her feel like she's dancing on air.

Ariel

Deep under the ocean in a beautiful watery kingdom there lived a little mermaid, named Princess Ariel. She was the youngest daughter of Triton, the Sea King and full of curiosity about the world outside the ocean. Ariel's greatest wish was to live like a human on dry land.

Daddy, I love him!

Unhappy princess

PRINCESS ARIEL IS A BEAUTIFUL MERMAID. She loves her father and older sisters, but she is not happy with her life underwater. She is determined to realize her dream of being a human on dry land, especially when she sets eyes upon handsome Prince Eric. Young and headstrong, Ariel usually gets her own way, but there is a price to pay.

Ariel loves to collect human objects she finds on sunken ships and the ocean floor. She stores her collection of treasures in a secret underwater grotto, close to the palace.

A telescope makes a good hat!

✶ Her favorite things

Ariel's best friend is a little fish named Flounder. They go on many exciting adventures together and often end up in lots of trouble!

Sebastian is Triton's loyal crab composer and is supposed to watch over Ariel. He tries hard but finds it difficult to keep up with her!

Ariel consults her funny seagull friend, Scuttle, about all human things. He claims to be an expert!

Her fins help her to swim fast.

Exploring

Even if it means swimming into dangerous, shark-infested waters, Ariel cannot resist the temptation to explore the ocean for shipwrecks so that she can add to her amazing collection of human things.

Her eyes are as blue as the ocean.

King Triton cannot understand his youngest daughter's love for humans. He thinks that they are dangerous and forbids her to go exploring.

Seashell bikini top

Ariel's hair is the color of red sea anemones and floats in the water.

The tiny scales on her tail shimmer like sequins.

I don't see how a world that makes such wonderful things could be bad!

About Ariel

- She's adventurous and curious.
- Headstrong and impulsive, Ariel refuses to listen to her father.
- She is romantic and gives up her voice for love.
- Ariel is funny and brave.

Under the sea

DEEP UNDER THE OCEAN is a marvelous world of brightly colored fish, corals and seaweeds, and a sparkling palace that is home to King Triton and his mermaid daughters. But danger lurks underwater too, if only Ariel would listen.

Ariel shares her bedroom with her six older sisters named Aquata, Andrina, Arista, Attina, Adella, and Alana. Sometimes Ariel finds it hard to be the youngest because everyone treats her like a child!

Ariel and her sisters' bedroom

King Triton loves Ariel dearly and is prepared to give up everything he has to save her from Ursula, the sea witch.

The underwater palace

King Triton's magnificent throne room

Treasures of the deep

Ariel is fascinated by all things from the human world, but she knows her father will be angry if he finds out about her secret collection.

She loves to examine the many objects in her cave and imagines what each thing is for.

Ursula

Ursula hates King Triton. The octopus-like sea witch longs to overthrow him so that she can become Queen of the Sea.

Ursula's spies, Flotsam and Jetsam, discover that Ariel is in love with Prince Eric and tell the sea witch. Ursula uses this to her advantage and offers Ariel a cruel deal.

Arches and tunnels are made from sea coral.

Giant clam shells make wonderful instruments in the concert hall.

On dry land

URSULA USES HER MAGIC TO MAKE ARIEL HUMAN and in exchange, Ariel gives up her beautiful voice. To stay human, Ariel must make Eric give her a kiss of true love within three days. If she fails, she will belong to Ursula. But Ariel doesn't realize that Ursula is up to no good and plans to use Ariel's voice to make Eric marry her! Luckily for Ariel, her friends and her father save the day.

 ## Prince Eric

Ariel sees Prince Eric for the first time as his magnificent ship sails past. It is the prince's birthday and the crew celebrates with fireworks.

A violent storm throws the prince overboard but Ariel rescues him and takes him to the shore. She falls deeply in love with Eric but cannot survive on land for long and quickly returns to the sea.

As soon as Ariel drinks Ursula's magic potion, her tail disappears and in its place are two legs. It takes Scuttle a while to work out what's different about her!

Ariel loves being able to walk through the town square, and enjoys talking to all the people.

In the castle kitchen, the chef is determined to catch Sebastian and serve him up for dinner!

Without a voice, it is difficult for Ariel to get the prince to fall in love with her and kiss her.

Roof-garden

Ariel's bedroom

The town

The sea view from the dining room means Ariel is never far from home.

Eric's ship

When King Triton sees how much Ariel and Prince Eric love each other, he allows them to get married.

Belle

A long time ago in France, a beggar woman asked a handsome prince for shelter from the cold, in return for a single rose. The selfish prince refused to help and the old woman (who was really an enchantress) turned him into a hideous Beast. The spell would only be broken if the prince learned to truly love another person.

You have my word.

A sweet girl

BELLE, WHOSE NAME MEANS BEAUTY IN FRENCH, knows that true beauty lies within. But even her goodness is tested when she first sets eyes on the hideous-looking beast who lives in the enchanted castle. Although she doesn't know it, Belle's loving nature and intelligence have the power to transform the Beast into a handsome prince who will make her his princess bride.

ABOUT BELLE

- She is loyal and gives up her freedom for the father she adores.
- She's clever and makes her own judgments.
- She is imaginative and loves to read stories.

I've just finished a wonderful story!

✳ Village friends

Belle's only true friends in the village are the heroes and heroines she meets in the books she loves to read.

Although some people in the village think that Maurice is just a crazy old man, Belle has total faith in her father.

Dancing in this stunning gown, she is truly Belle of the ball.

Her long silky hair is the color of chocolate.

Her big brown eyes are full of warmth.

The rose is a symbol of Belle's love for the Beast.

Castle friends

Lumiere and Cogsworth are two of the castle servants who are changed into household objects by the enchantress. They hope Belle will help them turn back into humans again.

Mrs. Potts, the kindly cook, and Chip, her playful son, cheer Belle up when she first arrives. They think that Belle is just the kind of girl to look beyond first appearances.

Special clothes

At the castle, the Wardrobe provides Belle with all the clothes she could possibly want.

Belle loves the beautiful fur-lined cloak that the Wardrobe gives her. She wears the cloak when she goes walking with the Beast in the beautiful snowy gardens. They have lots of fun playing in the snow and Belle realizes how nice the Beast really is.

Belle's world

BELLE LIVES WITH HER father in a quiet little town where nothing ever happens, and she longs for adventure and a little romance. She soon discovers that not far away lies an enchanted castle and a very different world.

Belle's house is on the outskirts of town, making her an outsider in more ways than one.

The head of the lunatic asylum calls to take Maurice away.

Gaston's admirers

No matter how hard they try, the three village girls cannot get Gaston to notice them. He only has eyes for the beautiful Belle.

The other girls in the village are not as pretty as Belle.

With her nose in a book all day long, Belle hardly notices the things that go on in the town around her. She dreams of a different life far, far away.

Maurice sets off for the fair
and rides unsuspectingly into
the spooky forest.

Which way? Maurice
gets lost when he
takes the wrong turn.

The Beast's castle

In the West Wing
Belle discovers the
enchanted rose.

The bookshop

The village
square and
fountain

The inn

Gaston
and the
villagers go
on the rampage
through the forest to
find the Beast and destroy him.

Inside the inn,
Gaston and Le Fou
plot how to capture
Belle's heart.

Learning to love

At first, Belle is desperately unhappy at being imprisoned in the castle, but soon learns to love the enchanted objects. Taming the bad-tempered Beast takes longer and what she doesn't know is that time is running out. The Beast must learn to love and be loved before the last petal of the enchanted rose falls or he will remain a Beast forever.

✳ Gaston and the Beast

Gaston may be handsome to look at, but when he proposes Belle is horrified at the thought of marrying such a vain and stupid man.

Belle is a beauty by nature as well as by name.

Belle loves her father so much that, although scared, she promises to stay in the Beast's castle forever so her father can be free.

Belle finds her evening meal is very entertaining!

The magical servants are overjoyed to welcome Belle to the enchanted castle. She is the first guest they have had for years!

His true nature

When the Beast learns to control his temper, Belle sees the kind and loving person within.

The Beast grants Belle her freedom so that she can help her father. This is a sign of his true love for her because he is willing to give up his only chance of becoming human again. This act of kindness makes Belle realize how much she loves him.

Belle manages to uncover the Beast's true nature.

The transformation

The Beast is terribly wounded by Gaston and Belle fears she is too late to save him. Tearfully she confesses her love for him and the spell is broken. The Beast regains his appearance as a handsome prince and all the enchanted objects become humans again.

Belle loves the Beast no matter what he looks like.

Jasmine

Brought up in a life of luxury in a far-off land, Princess Jasmine longed for adventure and excitement and the freedom to make her own choices. The last thing she wanted was to marry a silly, dull prince as the law and her father, the Sultan, said she must.

I am not a prize
to be won!

A sparkling sapphire is fixed upon her headband.

Eastern princess

PRINCESS JASMINE cannot bear being a princess. It's so boring! When she meets a street urchin named Aladdin, her life changes forever and she knows for sure that she could only marry someone she loves. Although her father and the evil Jafar have other plans for her, feisty Jasmine is not about to let them rule her life!

Her long, flowing hair is as smooth as satin.

💙 Likes

Jasmine's father is the Sultan of Agrabah and wants only the best for his daughter, including a prince for a husband.

She loves to wear her beautiful pink silk pants.

At first Abu is rude to Jasmine but she soon becomes very fond of the cheeky monkey.

Her chiffon wrap shimmers in the light.

Rajah is Jasmine's pet tiger and her closest friend in the palace. She tells him all her secrets and dreams.

Her slippers are made of gold.

♥ Dislikes

Jafar, the evil vizier and assistant to Jasmine's father, will never win her affection, no matter how powerful he is.

ABOUT JASMINE

Fiercely independent—she longs to be free and able to make her own choices. She's brave and isn't afraid to stand up to Jafar and speak her own mind! She's adventurous and intelligent.

If I do marry I want it to be for love.

Jasmine hates not being free to go where she chooses. She decides to see for herself what life is like on the other side of the palace walls.

Aladdin may be poor, but to Jasmine he is a prince.

Jasmine is not impressed when her father introduces her to Prince Ali because she doesn't recognize Aladdin in his princely clothes. Jasmine is determined to choose her own husband.

Agrabah

JASMINE LIVES IN THE DESERT CITY of Agrabah, in a splendid palace with her father. It is a wonderful city of mystery and enchantment, but she has never been outside the palace walls. Jasmine longs to experience the noise and excitement of the lively city for herself.

Hold on tight for a bird's eye view of Jasmine's world!

💜 The city

In the market place, the merchant isn't pleased when Jasmine gives an apple to a hungry child without realizing she should pay for it!

In the throne room, there is a hidden door that leads up to Jafar's secret lair. He goes there to think up ways to overthrow the Sultan.

The golden minarets glow in the sunlight.

Jafar's secret lair

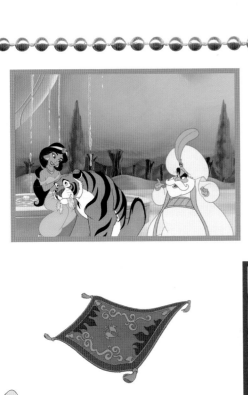

The Sultan's palace is surrounded by beautiful, exotic gardens. But even in these gardens Jasmine feels trapped and wants to see the city that lies beyond the palace walls.

Aladdin's secret hideaway is on the rooftop of an old, abandoned building. He has amazing views of the whole city and can even see the Sultan's palace.

The Sultan's palace

In the desert, on the outskirts of the city, the Cave of Wonders appears. The cave is filled with precious jewels and treasures. It is here that Aladdin finds the Magic Lamp.

The dungeon is located underneath the palace. This is where Aladdin is held after he is arrested by Jafar's men.

Eastern magic

IT MAY NOT LOOK LIKE much on the outside, but when Aladdin rubs the dirty old lamp, an all-powerful Genie appears. The Genie can grant his new master three wishes and could make Aladdin as powerful as the Sultan. But all Aladdin wants is to marry Jasmine—and in the end he doesn't need magic or the Genie to make her love him.

The Genie shows off his strength.

It feels good to be out after all those years inside the lamp!

The Genie has phenomenal cosmic powers.

The Genie

The Genie feels a little cramped inside the tiny lamp, his home for the last 10,000 years.

The Genie understands Jasmine's longing for freedom. Like her, he wants to be able to make his own choices and be his own master. Although the Genie is powerful, he can only grant other people's wishes—not his own.

The Magic Carpet can fly faster than the wind!

Jasmine loves to see the world by air.

Iago is Jafar's noisy, bad-tempered parrot.

🤍 The Magic Carpet

Stuck in the Cave of Wonders, Aladdin and Abu might never have escaped if it were not for the Magic Carpet. Although shy and timid at first, the Carpet becomes their friend and helps them escape from danger.

Aladdin's first wish is that he be turned into the wealthy Prince Ali. After Jafar has been defeated, Aladdin has his final wish. He asks that the Genie be set free from the lamp.

Jafar steals the Magic Lamp and the Genie is forced to obey his evil wishes. Aladdin knows that Jafar craves power, and cleverly tricks him into wishing to be a genie. Jafar's wish comes true and he becomes trapped in the lamp forever.

May all your wishes come true!

Mulan

A long, long time ago in Ancient China there lived a young girl named Mulan. She was a kind and loving daughter, but Mulan had an unfortunate habit of causing trouble without meaning to. She longed to find a path that would bring happiness and make her parents proud.

You don't meet a girl like that every dynasty.

A special girl

MULAN KNOWS THAT she will never be refined and graceful like the other girls, but she tries hard to please her family. She looks after her father, helps around the home by feeding the chickens, and tries not to cause too much trouble.

Loving family

Mulan's mother and grandmother think she should get married and take her to see a matchmaker. If the matchmaker likes Mulan she will help her make a good marriage.

ABOUT MULAN
♥ She's kind and caring, but also a little clumsy and accident prone!
♥ She loves her family more than anything and will do anything to make them happy.
♥ She's brave and clever.

Although Mulan is not happy to be meeting the matchmaker, she tries her best because she loves her family. She manages to look elegant, but soon spoils the pretty picture by dancing the wrong steps and then accidentally setting the matchmaker on fire!

Hair that just won't stay neat!

Belt to make her waist look tiny.

Simple style of dress

At home Mulan's best friends are a horse and dog, who look out for her and help her with the chores.

When Mulan starts her journey some new friends accompany her—Mushu the dragon and the lucky Cri-kee.

Family honor

Mulan longs to bring honor to her family but doesn't know how. When her father is called up to fight in the army, Mulan thinks he is too sick to make the trip.

It's going to take a miracle to get into the army.

In the middle of the night, Mulan steals her father's armor and sword so that she can take his place in the army. She disguises herself as a boy named Ping and sets off on a crazy adventure.

Finding herself

MULAN WANTS TO SAVE her father but joining the army is no picnic, nor is pretending to be a smelly man! But Mulan is determined to succeed and bring honor to her family. Although she has Mushu and Cri-kee by her side, her fellow new recruits don't seem very friendly.

Dangerous times

China is under threat from the invading Huns so the Emperor calls up every available male into the army. The Emperor is a wise and great man but his advisor Chi Fu is not so smart.

At first Mulan's fellow soldiers don't seem to like "Ping" very much, but "his" courage and strength win them over. Eventually!

The soldiers are led by Captain Li Shang. He is tough and brave and wants his men to be just like him.

Mulan has to prove to Shang that "Ping" has what it takes to be a good soldier. Through hard work and perseverance she shows him she can do it.

Beautiful headdress

The Huns are led by the ruthless Shan Yu. However, Mulan's quick thinking saves first Shang and then the Emperor.

The Emperor is proud of Mulan and honors her with a medal and a sword.

Mulan is able to return home with honor and pride. Her father is just happy to see her!

Ornate, jewel-encrusted sleeves

Beautifully patterned garment worn over dress

Simple dress underneath

Happy at last

Mulan has found both happiness and honor and she is delighted to be home. After some wise words from the Emperor, Shang goes to see Mulan—and even her grandmother approves of him!

Pocahontas

*M*any years ago in what was then known by many people as the New World, a free-spirited girl longed for adventure. Her name was Pocahontas and her dreams seemed to be telling her that something amazing would happen to her soon, but her father wanted her to settle down and get married.

This is the path I choose.

Free spirit

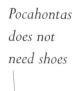
Long dark hair that blows in the wind

POCAHONTAS IS A MEMBER of the Powhatan tribe. She loves roaming the beautiful lands around her village and dreams of great adventures just around the corner. Her father is the Chief and he thinks his carefree daughter should settle down and marry the tribe's bravest warrior, Kocoum.

This necklace belonged to Pocahontas' mother

Family ties

Pocahontas' father is an important man. He must take care of the whole tribe and make difficult decisions.

When Pocahontas needs advice, she visits Grandmother Willow. The ancient talking tree is extremely wise.

Simple dress made of animal skins

The Powhatan tribe care for and respect the land they live on. They will do anything they can to keep it safe.

Pocahontas does not need shoes

Nakoma is Pocahontas' very best friend.

Pocahontas' best friends

Although Pocahontas is a free spirit she has some special friends, including a racoon named Meeko and tiny bird named Flit.

Meeko and Flit look out for Pocahontas.

Kocoum is a handsome warrior, but also very serious.

Flit is always hungry!

ABOUT POCAHONTAS

♥ Stubborn and independent, she doesn't want to marry Kocoum.

♥ Pocahontas means "little mischief".

♥ She is also brave enough to stand up for what she believes in.

It seems that Pocahontas is right, an amazing change is coming. English adventurer Captain John Smith is sailing to the New World to find gold and other riches. But he may not find a warm welcome from the Powhatan tribe.

John Smith finds something more valuable than gold when he meets Pocahontas—true love!

Against the odds

At FIRST POCAHONTAS and John Smith do not trust each other. By listening to their hearts they soon begin to understand each other better and it is not long before they realize that they are falling in love. But they know they must keep their feelings hidden from their friends and families.

John Smith and Pocahontas are not the only ones who are making new friends. When Meeko meets Governor Ratcliffe's pampered pet dog, Percy, the unlikely pair become pals!

 Greedy visitor

John Smith is working for Governor Ratcliffe, a greedy man who just wants wealth and power. He believes that Pocahontas and her tribe are hiding lots of valuable gold.

When Pocahontas and John Smith's romance becomes public, it very nearly leads to tragedy. First Pocahontas saves John Smith's life, then John saves her father from the Governor's bullet.

♥ *Tough goodbye*

John Smith takes the bullet meant for the Chief and very nearly loses his own life. He must return home if he is to survive.

Long hair arranged in elegant "up" do

Pocahontas bids farewell to John Smith, knowing they will never forget each other.

Elegant lace cuffs

Pretty gold bows

Beautiful full skirt

Tiana

*I*n 1920s New Orleans, a young waitress
dreamed of owning her own restaurant.
Her name was Tiana. Hard-working Tiana
didn't have much time for fun or romance—
she was too busy holding down two jobs and
saving up her money. However, a masquerade
ball would launch Tiana into an adventure
that would change her life forever.

I DO NOT kiss frogs!

Busy girl

A<small>MBITIOUS AND HARD WORKING,</small> Tiana knows exactly what she wants to do with her life—run her own restaurant. However, that means working two jobs to save up enough money to make her dream come true. That doesn't leave her with much time to relax!

This crown is only pretend

 ## Daddy's girl

Food has always been an important part of Tiana's life, thanks to her father James.

Tiana is wearing one of Charlotte's many dresses

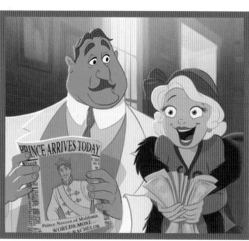

Tiana's best friend is Charlotte LaBouff. The two girls' lives couldn't be more different— Charlotte's Daddy gets her everything she wants.

ABOUT TIANA

♥ Busy Tiana doesn't have time for parties.

♥ Tiana has been best friends with Charlotte since they were little girls

♥ Unlike her friend, Tiana doesn't dream of marrying a handsome prince.

 ## *Important visitor*

Prince Naveen of Maldonia is the complete opposite of Tiana—he loves parties and has never done a day's work in his life! His greatest passion is jazz and he has come to New Orleans to make sweet music, and hopefully find a rich woman to marry!

Prince Naveen's parents are tired of their son's party lifestyle so they disinherit him. The pampered prince needs to find a way to get some money. Working for it is out of the question, of course.

Prince Naveen is the guest of honor at Charlotte's father's masquerade ball. Charlotte hopes he will fall in love with her. Tiana is just there to work.

A froggy business

TIANA IS NOT interested in princes and fairy tales, that's Charlotte's dream. However, it is Tiana, not Charlotte, who finds herself caught up in a truly amazing story. A prince with a problem, some quirky creatures, and a sprinkling of magic are the recipe for adventure.

I'm not a princess.
I'm a waitress.

At Charlotte's ball, Tiana's outfit gets ruined so she borrows one of Charlotte's dresses. When Naveen sees her, he thinks that he has found his princess and begs her for a kiss.

 ## Prince charmed

Dr. Facilier promises to make Prince Naveen rich, but the mean magician turns him into a frog instead! He tells him that only a kiss from a princess can break the spell.

The kiss doesn't quite go as planned and Tiana becomes a frog too! The froggy pair make a quick escape from the party and head to the bayou.

Ray is a romantic firefly who shows the froggy pair that anything is possible, if it's true love.

Life as frogs isn't easy, but Naveen and Tiana make some good friends in the bayou. Louis is a jazz-loving alligator with a heart of gold.

Tiana and Naveen grow closer in the bayou as their adventure shows them what really matters in life.

 ## *True love*

It's certainly not love at first sight, but as Tiana teaches Naveen about hard work, he teaches her about the other important things in life.

Magical Mama Odie tells them that to be happy, and become human again, they must find out what they need, not what they want.

Tiana's Palace

TIANA'S LOVE OF cooking began when she was a little girl and she used to cook bowls of gumbo with her father. Now she works as a waitress, saving up all her money until she can buy her own place. When that day comes, Tiana will use everything she has learned to make her restaurant the best in town.

Big dreams

Tiana first dreamt of having her own restaurant when she was a little girl and shared her plans with her father, James. He always encouraged her to follow her dreams.

Tiana works the day shift at Duke's Diner and the night shift at Cal's. She is a busy girl!

Customers can be very demanding, but Tiana is a good waitress and knows how to do lots of things at once!

Dreams come true

After a lot of hard work and a little bit of magic, Tiana finally opens her own place. And with Naveen by her side, it is even better than she dreamed it would be!

At Tiana's restaurant everyone is welcome— kings, queens, and her new friends from the bayou!

When she was a child, Tiana dreamed of calling her restaurant *Tiana's Place*. Now she is grown up, and a princess, she thinks *Tiana's Palace* is a better name!

Princess Tiana

TIANA AND NAVEEN get to know each other as frogs and eventually realize that they can't live without each other. When it seems like they might never be human again, the perfect pair decide that just being together is enough for them.

 ## Tough choice

Tiana and Naveen are ruining Dr. Facilier's schemes. He offers Tiana a restaurant, if she will betray Naveen. But Tiana finally understands what she needs.

Naveen has learned what he needs too—Tiana. And he would do anything for her.

Charlotte knows true love when she sees it and offers to kiss Naveen to break the spell. But she is too late.

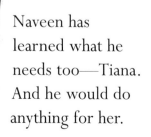

Tiana and Naveen believe that they will have to remain frogs forever and decide to get married. When they kiss as husband and wife, the spell breaks—Tiana is a real princess now!

 ## New dream

Tiana never dreamed of becoming a princess, but she certainly likes being one now! As for Naveen, a little time as a frog makes him a much better prince.

After their froggy wedding, Tiana and Naveen have a human one too. Their family and friends all join them to celebrate, and Charlotte catches Tiana's bouquet!

Rapunzel

*O*nce upon a time, a girl with long blonde hair lived in a tall tower. The girl's name was Rapunzel and she was a princess. However, Rapunzel was kidnapped by a wicked woman when she was a baby and she had no idea who she really was...

I've been looking out of a window for *eighteen years*.

Hidden

RAPUNZEL HAS spent the last eighteen years living inside a tower. She believes that Gothel is her mother and has no idea that she is really a princess. But on her eighteenth birthday, Rapunzel's life changes forever.

Simple, homemade dress

 ## Young princess

The King and Queen loved their daughter very much and have been very sad since she was stolen. Every year on her birthday they release lanterns in her memory.

Long, magical hair

Gothel stole Rapunzel as a baby. The princess's hair contains magic that keeps Gothel looking young and beautiful.

When I promise something, I never ever break that promise.

Keeping busy

Gothel doesn't let Rapunzel leave the tower—ever—so the energetic young girl has to find ways to amuse herself.

ABOUT RAPUNZEL

♥ Her hair is 70 feet (21 meters) long. It takes three hours to brush her hair and six hours to wash it!

♥ Her favorite color is lavender.

Rapunzel likes to keep fit, but it is no substitute for the feeling of grass beneath her feet.

One of Rapunzel's favorite hobbies is painting.

The secret tower

GOTHEL HAS HIDDEN Rapunzel well. The scheming lady chose a secret tower in the middle of a mysterious valley. It has no front door so Gothel uses Rapunzel's long hair as a ladder when she wants to get in or out of the tower. For eighteen years no one has found them, until now...

✿ Visitor

Lovable rogue Flynn Rider is being chased when he stumbles upon the tower. He thinks it will be a great place to hide.

Window from which Rapunzel lets down her hair

Flynn climbs the outside of the tower and Rapunzel welcomes him with a frying pan!

✾ Free at last

At first Rapunzel is suspicious of Flynn, until she realizes he can help her leave the tower. Finally, Rapunzel is going to see what is out there!

Gothel has never told Rapunzel, but there is a trapdoor in the floor hiding a secret staircase. It leads to the outside world.

New people

RAPUNZEL HAS LED a very sheltered life. The only person she sees is Mother Gothel, and her only friend is a chameleon named Pascal. However, when Flynn Rider enters her life Rapunzel meets a lot more people. Not all of them are nice.

Maximus is a horse with the Palace Guard. He is strong and brave, but a pushover for Rapunzel's sweet-talking.

Friends

Pascal can't talk but he changes color to reflect his mood. He is a loyal friend to Rapunzel.

The regulars at the Snuggly Duckling look scary, but they all have a dream, just like Rapunzel.

At first Flynn's charms don't work on Rapunzel but later they grow to like each other. Flynn even risks his life to save Rapunzel.

Enemies

The Stabbington brothers are double trouble. The twins help Gothel find Rapunzel, but they are really looking for Flynn Rider.

Rapunzel is not used to the outside world, but she can't stay locked in a tower forever, no matter what Gothel thinks!

Gothel will stop at nothing to keep Rapunzel and her magical hair all to herself.

Without Rapunzel's hair, Gothel starts to look her age.

Home at last

Leaving the tower is the best thing that has ever happened to Rapunzel. She is finally free to make new friends, fall in love, and—best of all—go home to her real parents.

Something special

Flynn helps Rapunzel enjoy her best-ever birthday. She realizes that he is a special person.

In the outside world, Rapunzel's hair can get in a tangle, so she finds a stylish way to keep it out of the way.

✤ *Magic lanterns*

Rapunzel has always wanted to see the beautiful lanterns that are released every year on her birthday.

Rapunzel eventually realizes that the lanterns are for her!

I'm the lost princess.

To save Rapunzel from Gothel, Flynn cuts off Rapunzel's magical hair.

✤ Reunited

The King and Queen are overjoyed to have their beloved daughter back. Rapunzel is happy to be a princess again.

Happy ending

THE ROYAL ADVENTURES are at an end. Snow White, Aurora, Cinderella, Ariel, Belle, Jasmine, Mulan, Pocahontas, Tiana, and Rapunzel have all learned that being a princess is not as easy as you might think. Bad spells have been broken, new friendships have been made, challenges have been faced, and, of course, true love has been found. It's time for all the princesses to go and live happily ever after.

DK

LONDON, NEW YORK, MELBOURNE,
MUNICH, AND DELHI

DESIGNERS *Cathy Tincknell, Lisa Lanzarini, and Lisa Sodeau*
SENIOR EDITOR *Lindsay Kent*
DESIGN MANAGER *Ron Stobbart*
PUBLISHING MANAGER *Catherine Saunders*
ART DIRECTOR *Lisa Lanzarini*
PUBLISHER *Simon Beecroft*
PUBLISHING DIRECTOR *Alex Allan*
PRE-PRODUCTION PRODUCER *Siu Chan*
SENIOR PRODUCER *Shabana Shakir*
ADDITIONAL ART *Marco Colletti, Silvano Scolari, and Vincenzo Genna*
JACKET DESIGN *Satvir Sihota*

First published in the United States in 2003 and revised in 2008.
This revised edition published in 2012 by
DK Publishing, 375 Hudson Street, New York, New York 10014

10 9 8 7 6 5 4 3 2 1
001—184088—Oct/12

DK books are available at special discounts when purchased in bulk for
sales promotions, premiums, fund-raising, or educational use.
For details, contact: DK Publishing Special Markets, 375 Hudson
Street, New York, New York 10014. SpecialSales@dk.com

ISBN 978-0-7566-9798-3

Color reproduction by MDP, UK
Printed and bound at Hung Hing, China.

Discover more at
www.dk.com